# TIPPING TOWARD BALANCE

A Fitness Trainer's Guide
To Stability And Walking

By Tracy L. Markley. C.P.T.
Biomechanics Specialist

No part of this publication may be reproduced, stored in a retrieval system, or transmitted in any form or by any means, electronic, photocopying, recording, or otherwise without prior written permission, except in the case of brief excerpts in critical reviews and articles. For permission requests, contact the author at tracy@tracyspersonaltraining.com.

All rights reserved.
Copyright © 2018 Tracy L. Markley

ISBN-13: 978-1986552813
ISBN-10: 1986552810

The author disclaim responsibility for adverse effects or consequences from the misapplication or injudicious use of the information contained in this book. Mention of resources and associations does not imply an endorsement.

Cover design:
Book layout design & eBook conversion by manuscript2ebook.com

Dedicated to Essie
Thank you for your kindness,
your inspiration,
and the lovely memories.

# TABLE OF CONTENTS

**Foreword by Greg Justice** .......................................... 1

**Introduction** .................................................................. 5

**Chapter One** ................................................................. 7
   Spatial Awareness and Feeling Safe in Movement

**Chapter Two** .............................................................. 11
   Why These Muscles are Important for Balance

**Chapter Three** ........................................................... 27
   Tripping on Roots and Falling

**Chapter Four** ............................................................. 31
   Bruns-Garland Syndrome

**Chapter Five** .............................................................. 35
   Foot Pain and Fascial Issues

**Chapter Six** ................................................................ 39
   Another Tripper

**Chapter Seven** ............................................................. 41
    Stroke Survivors

**Chapter Eight** ............................................................. 47
    Scoliosis

**Chapter Nine** .............................................................. 53
    A Letter From a 90-Year-Old Client

**Chapter Ten** ................................................................ 57
    105-Year-Old Gains Core Strength

**Chapter Eleven** ........................................................... 61
    Feeling Uncoordinated, Kids and Teens

**Chapter Twelve** .......................................................... 65
    Balance Disc - BOSU® Ball - Swiss Ball

**Chapter Thirteen** ........................................................ 69
    Hearing Loss Linked to Falls

**Chapter Fourteen** ....................................................... 73
    8 Exercises for Balance and Stability in Movement

**Acknowledgements** ................................................. 105

# FOREWORD
## by Greg Justice

I have known Tracy for a few years through my service to an industry for which I have great passion. I see that same passion in Tracy through the work she does with her clients. As a fitness professional myself, and the co-founder of Scriptor Publishing Group, I've had the opportunity to coach, train, and guide many clients toward their vision of success ... I like to say, "I'm in the business of making dreams come true." For many of Tracy's clients, that 'dream' is an enhanced quality of life because of chronic pain, disease, or lack of conditioning.

# TIPPING TOWARD BALANCE

Early in the book, Tracy covers the topic of spatial awareness. She gives a wonderful example of a client who regained his awareness by working with Tracy, and the joy she felt by being part of his success. It's important to understand the impact we can have on others through our chosen profession, and the satisfaction of changing lives for the better.

As the book progresses, Tracy talks about the importance of balance and the muscles needed for a healthier balancing system. Another great example is given when she talks about an overweight client who came to her because he was tripping and falling down at work … it just happened that he worked in the rainforest and was tripping on tree roots on hiking trails. After doing Tracy's protocol, he regained his strength and balance and wasn't falling anymore.

Throughout the book, Tracy shares many more success stories. She's helped clients with Bruns-Garland syndrome, scoliosis, and even stroke victims, but perhaps my favorite is the 104-year-old lady who

## FOREWORD

regained strength, balance and spatial awareness while working with Tracy.

Tracy's workout system is covered in thorough detail in chapter 14 in what she calls "Eight Exercises for Balance and Stability in Movement". I especially appreciated the detailed explanation of each of the exercises.

In her first book, *The Stroke of An Artist*, Tracy offered hope, inspiration and encouragement to stroke recovery patients and their families. This book offers that same hope, inspiration and encouragement to those suffering from many other conditions, syndromes, and ailments, and offers a proven method to enhance their quality of life, through safe, personalized exercise.

# INTRODUCTION

In this book I share eight exercises and the reasons why they have helped clients regain their balance. These particular exercises have helped clients stop tripping and falling and to regain the ability to feel safe in movement again. I also share some short stories of clients who all have various reasons for losing their balance.

A range of personal and specific factors may play a role in the body's balance and walking gait as they become off-kilter. This leaves people feeling unsafe in their movements, which, in turn, causes the walking gait to change and slow down because they feel out of balance or unstable. At this point, individuals may find themselves tripping often and/or falling down.

At any age, but often as we get older, the body can become weaker. That can be due to illness, lack of exercise, neurological challenges or a diagnosed condition. In many of these cases, the body begins to move more slowly. You can feel unsafe in everyday movements, even just walking. The center of the body, known as the core, must be built up in strength for the rest of the body to be able to perform movements at their best. Frequently, building core strength is thought to be achievable only when you get down on the floor and do crunches. Many clients with weakness or stability issues do not feel safe getting down to the floor. Consequently, that leaves them thinking it is a lost cause to attempt to strengthen the core muscles. Thankfully, this is not the truth.

CHAPTER ONE

# SPATIAL AWARENESS AND FEELING SAFE IN MOVEMENTS

Spatial awareness is the ability to be conscious of oneself in space, to be mindful of where your body's location is, the amount of room you have around it, and to have knowledge of the distance of objects within your surroundings. It is also referred to as proprioception - the placement of the body in relation to the things around it. It is the discernment of organized knowledge of the objects around oneself, in relation to the given space at any time, either when being still, or when there is a change of position. It relates to the height and depth of the objects around you. For example, stepping over something on the floor when you are walking through a room requires that you must be able to relate to the height of the object you need to step over. That way your foot lifts high enough, and steps out far enough, before landing back on the floor in order to clear the object. Many of my clients have tripped over roots on the ground on hiking trails, leading them to stop hiking the beautiful trails they love. Spatial awareness is a complex cognitive skill which we learn as children. It must be relearned in many cases, as discussed in this book.

Without adequate proprioception from the trunk and legs, it is difficult even to walk into a room and sit down in a chair. For example, when you enter a room and are aware of the chair's distance, the brain calculates the distance and the feet walk accordingly. The body starts taking smaller steps when needed, as well as adjusting the speed of each step as it approaches the chair to turn around. Now the brain calculates the turn, the size of steps required, and their direction

## SPATIAL AWARENESS AND FEELING SAFE IN MOVEMENTS

in order to place the body in the right position to prepare to sit. It then calculates the distance, height, and location of the seat of the chair in space as it coordinates with the body's location in space, before it lowers the body to sit down safely. The brain directs the body so that it knows where it is in space in order to guide it down into sitting position in the chair, without missing the chair and falling to the floor. There is a re-enactment video of this on my YouTube channel listed on my website with a client who rebuilt this ability. (www.tracyspersonaltraining.com)

One day I was training a client, and out of the blue, he explained to me that he knew there was the road with cars driving on it outside the gym, and that there were people around him in the gym, but only because he knew it, not because he "saw" or "felt" them around him. The sense of his surroundings was not there. He was actually describing his loss of spatial awareness. This particular client was incredibly in tune, and his explanation was amazing.

One day, several months later, he was standing on the balance disc. He stepped off the disc and said, "Wait, I need to share something." He made a small movement with his arms close to his body as if he were making a small circle around himself with his hands and said, "It is like my world used to stop here." Then he reached his arms and hands out as far as he could, making a large circle around his body, then said, "But now it ends here." I felt such joy for him. It was fascinating. The way he explained it felt magical. I said to myself, "Wow, he just got his awareness back. This is phenomenal!"

Then I thought, "Oh my God, I helped him achieve that."

I was joyfully overwhelmed. It remains one of my favorite and most powerful moments in my fitness career.

CHAPTER TWO

# WHY THESE MUSCLES ARE IMPORTANT FOR BALANCE

We all want to feel stable and safe in movement. I feel knowledge is power. In this chapter, I highlight some of the principles that I have found to be the foundations of strengthening the muscles needed for a healthier balancing system in the body. This is the most complex, but also a very important chapter in this book. It is written for those who need to improve their balance and stability, and to regain the awareness of their body's location in space. It is also a good resource for professionals who work with clients with these needs.

## TIPPING TOWARD BALANCE

I have obtained knowledge from some great teachers in the past 20 years while working in the fitness industry. My teaching methods are a combination of knowledge from all of these teachers, as well as my experience with my clients. I have trained clients of all ages, ranging from 5 to 105.

Scientific research has shown that in a healthy body, the brain sends a message to specific muscles in the core of the body before it sends a message to the legs and the arms for movement. This is the brain telling these muscles to stabilize and support the body, because it is ready to move. I like to call this the balancing system of the body. With this in mind, for example, if a client has had a stroke, the brain is already having a hard time getting messages to the body for proper movement. The brain is trying to create new pathways of communication because the old pathways are not working properly. It makes sense to me that if the stabilizing muscles are weak, and not functioning to their full potential, it could

## WHY THESE MUSCLES ARE IMPORTANT FOR BALANCE

cause the rebuilding of pathways to the limbs to be more difficult to achieve.

If the core of the body is strong, it can stabilize better, so the limbs can become stronger, and work in better movement with the body as a team, like they were made to do. It is also important to understand that each muscle in the body has a specific job to do in moving the body. If some muscles are too weak to perform the job they were meant to do, other muscles try to do their job for them. This is like a sport team with players that can't play the sport very well. It throws the whole team off.

There is less stress on the body physiologically when the biomechanics are functioning properly. Physiology focuses on the systems and organs of the body and their functions.

The **transverse abdominal muscle**, the **multifidus muscle**, **diaphragm**, and the **pelvic floor muscles** are all on the same neuromuscular loop. This means it's best if all those muscles are functioning properly. Each needs to perform its job individually <u>and</u> as a team. If the transverse muscle is weak, the pelvic floor, the multifidus, and the diaphragm cannot gain proper strength to perform their job for a healthy, functioning body.

The transverse muscle is the deepest of the abdominal muscles. A critical function of this muscle is to stabilize the lower back and pelvis before movement. It is the deepest abdominal muscle, wrapping around the body to act like a corset. When engaged, it also pulls the belly in and provides support to the thoracolumbar fascia. It is the main stabilizer of the shoulder girdle, the head, neck, pelvis, and lower extremities.

If a client has rounded shoulders and poor posture, it will not be corrected if the transverse muscle maintains the weakness. The transverse muscle needs to be strengthened, along with the other stabilizing muscles, to hold the body strongly upright so that it can achieve a posture in which the shoulders are stacked over the hips. If the head is upright and balanced over the shoulders, we have better balance.

## WHY THESE MUSCLES ARE IMPORTANT FOR BALANCE

Clients need to rebuild stability in the pelvis and hips, so that the lower limbs and joints can gain strength, function in alignment, and perform properly for safe movements.

The multifidus is a small but powerful muscle. It is the main stabilizing muscle of the spine. This muscle takes pressure off the vertebral discs so that the body weight can be distributed throughout the spine. If this is weak, you will also have weakness in the low back. The multifidus begins to activate before the body moves to protect the spine. It is part of the stabilizing system in the body. In order to gain better balance this muscle must be stronger. Performing various exercises combined with the Swiss ball, balance disc and BOSU® ball will help gain a stronger multifidus. Better posture leads to better balance.

The small muscles near the vertebrae need to be activated harmoniously. These muscles are postural muscles. Exercising on an unstable surface, such as the Swiss ball, balance disc and the BOSU® ball, stimulates the central nervous system which is the brain and the spinal cord. It strengthens muscles and ligaments, as well as activating and strengthening all the small muscles along the spinal column.

The pelvic floor muscles work as stabilizers of the abdominal and pelvic organs. The pelvic floor muscles and the gluteus (buttock) muscles are made to work and move in opposite directions. One must be able to engage the pelvic floor without engaging the gluteus muscles in order to obtain optimal core strength. This plays a role in preventing back issues, and I don't want to build back issues in any client. The transverse muscle must be strong in order for the pelvic floor to become strong and function properly, since they are on the same neuromuscular loop.

The pelvic floor works closely with the diaphragm as well. If you sit or stand in good alignment and focus on engaging the pelvic floor, you can feel that the diaphragm pulls slightly towards the pelvic floor as the pelvic floor lifts slightly upwards towards the diaphragm. There is a difference between doing a Kegel and engaging the pelvic floor. It is important

## WHY THESE MUSCLES ARE IMPORTANT FOR BALANCE

to be able to engage the pelvic floor without engaging the buttocks for the stabilizing system in the body to work efficiently.

When clients do these specific eight exercises, I tell them to engage the pelvic floor then to visualize, and feel, as if they are putting on a snug girdle or a corset, by zipping up a zipper from their pubic bone to the top of their rib cage. This sensation usually puts the body into proper posture. The more conscious and present a client is when doing this, the better the chance, subconsciously, of these muscles contracting in everyday movements when needed. It is important to remember to keep this focus throughout the exercises in this book.

The **psoas muscle** is an extremely important muscle located in the center of the body. It lies deep underneath the transverse abdominal muscle. It is a deep back muscle. Often it is referred to as the iliopsoas. This is when the psoas and the iliacus muscle are being grouped together. The psoas muscle is the only muscle in the back that crosses over the hips and attaches at the front of the body. It attaches at the last thoracic vertebrae and to four of the five lumbar vertebrae, and at the femur, the upper thigh bone. If the psoas is short, weak and/or tight it will be difficult to hold the body in an upright position with the shoulders stacked over the hips.

As you look at the muscle illustrations in this chapter, you will gain a better understanding of how important it is to have the center of the body, strong and stable. Our bodies need all these muscles to be strong and working together as a team for proper movement. Achieving a balanced body and walking gait will lead to being safer in movement.

To sum this chapter up, proper posture and sitting up tall does not begin at the shoulders. Let's strengthen from deep in the core to help straighten up. The center of the body must be strong to hold up the diaphragm, rib cage and shoulder girdles in proper alignment in order to have proper posture.

Holding your body upright in a proper posture, not only looks better, and helps the body to balance

## WHY THESE MUSCLES ARE IMPORTANT FOR BALANCE

better, it makes the systems in the body work and function better.

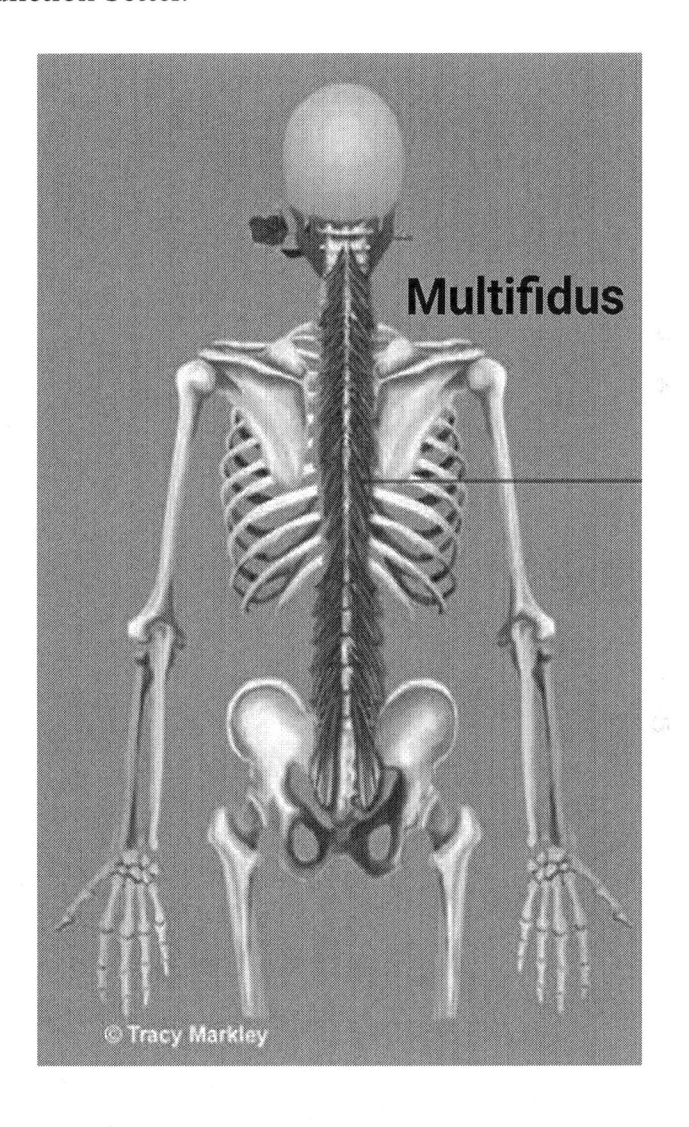

**Multifidus**

© Tracy Markley

Transverse

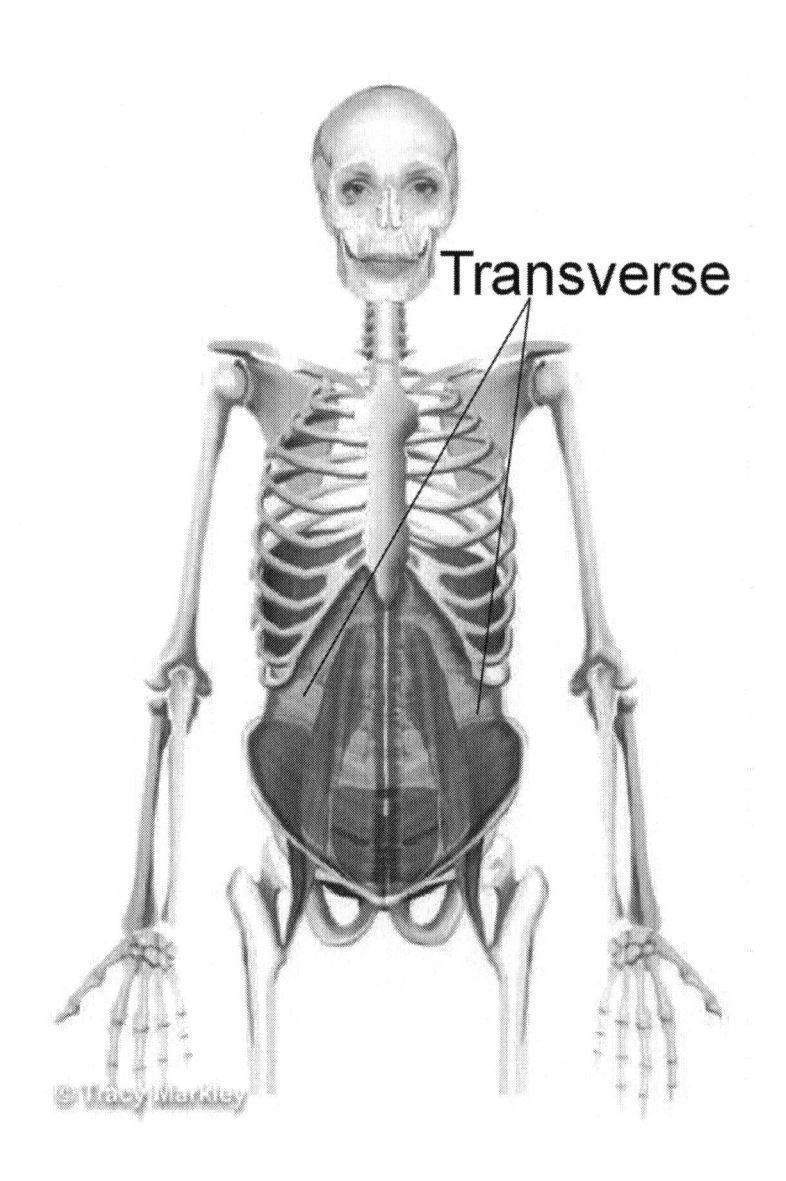

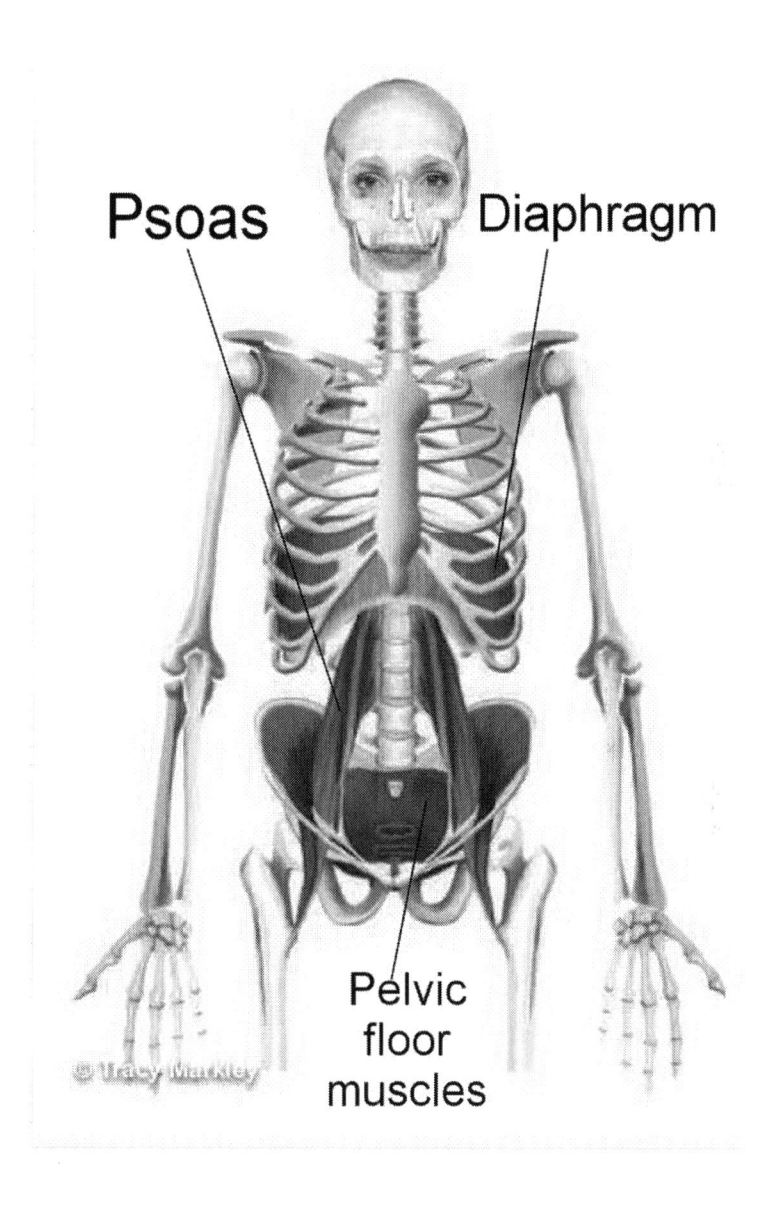

# WHY THESE MUSCLES ARE IMPORTANT FOR BALANCE

21

TIPPING TOWARD BALANCE

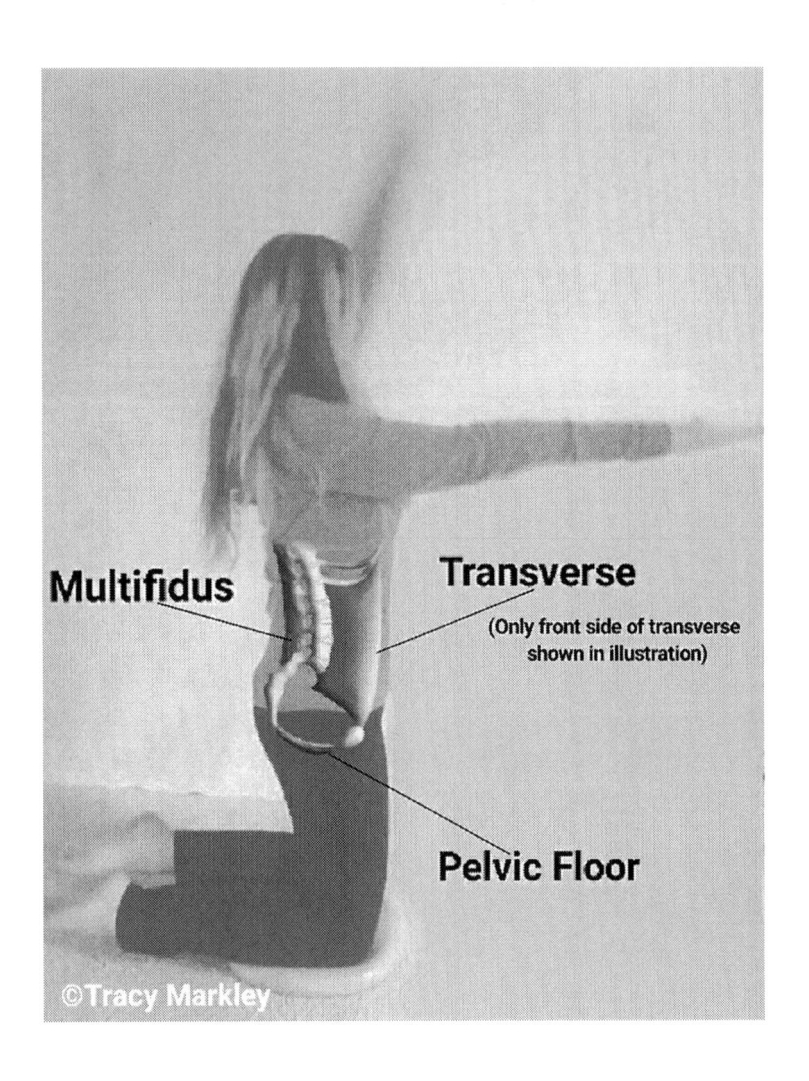

**Multifidus** **Transverse**
(Only front side of transverse shown in illustration)

**Pelvic Floor**

©Tracy Markley

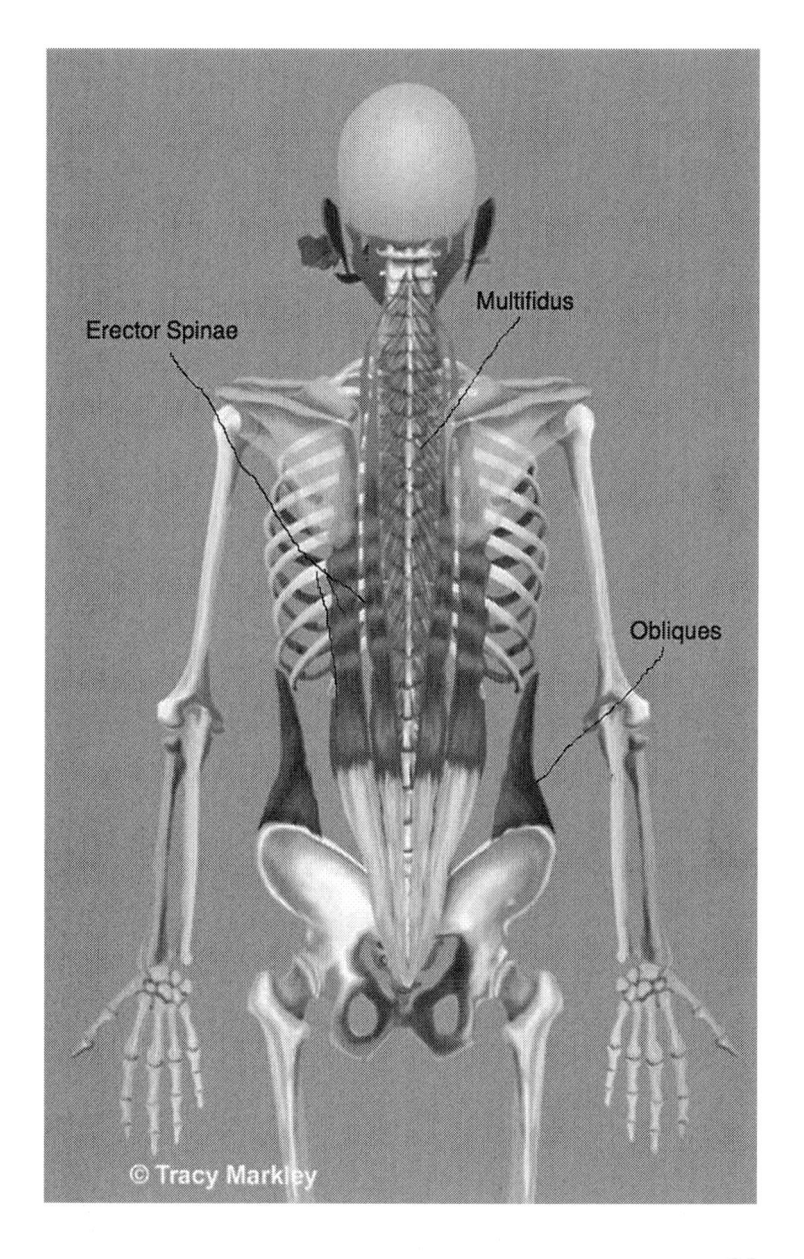

# WHY THESE MUSCLES ARE IMPORTANT FOR BALANCE

# TIPPING TOWARD BALANCE

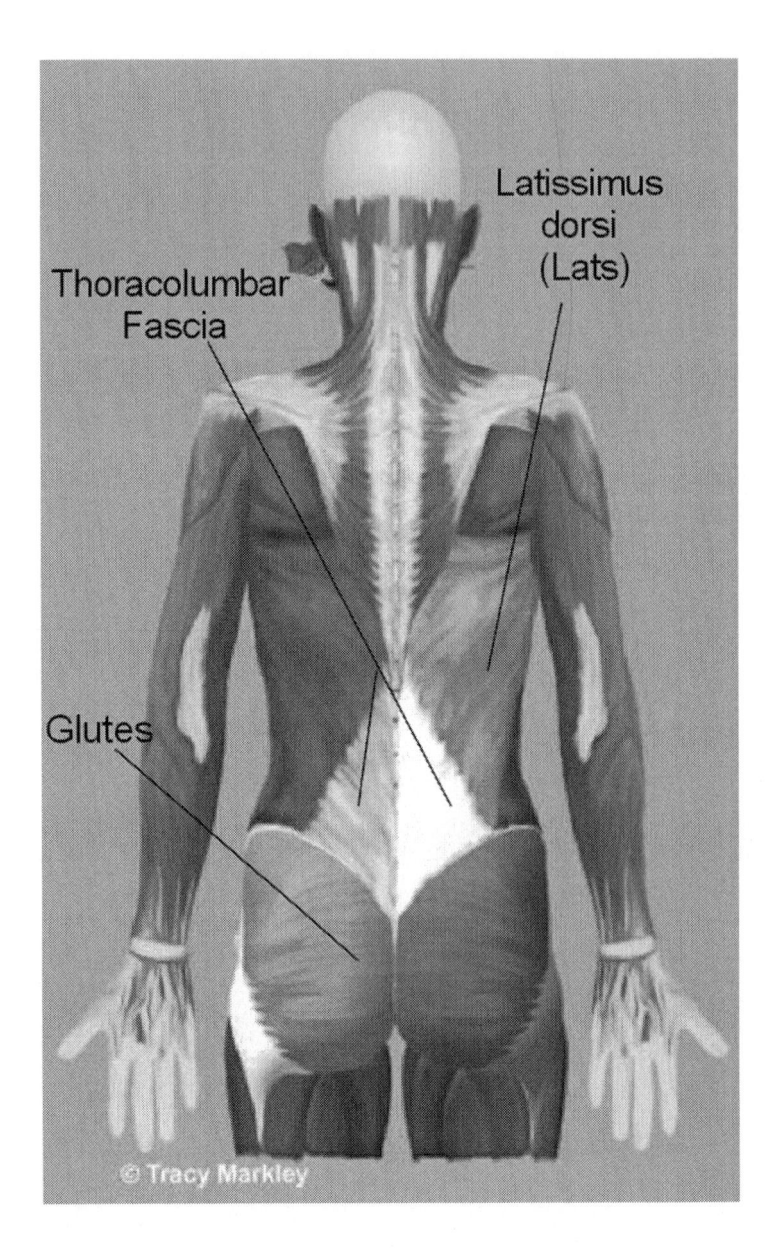

# WHY THESE MUSCLES ARE IMPORTANT FOR BALANCE

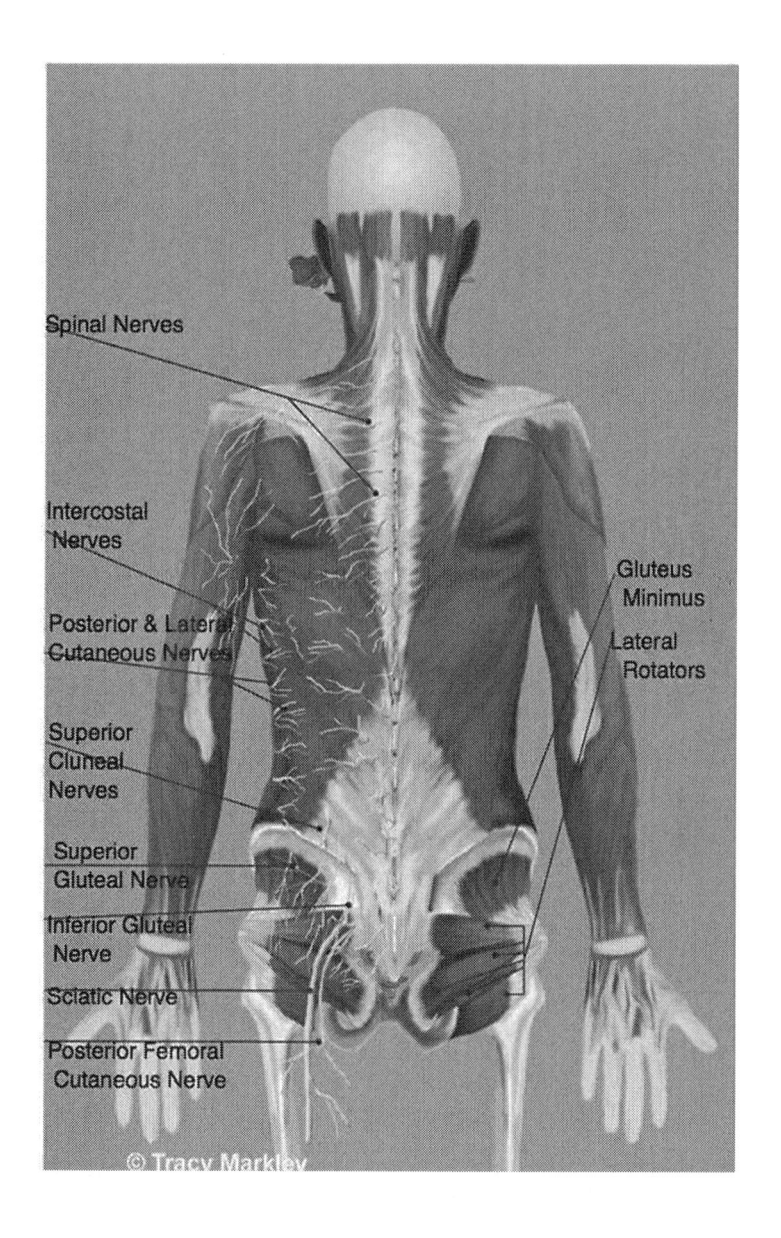

- Spinal Nerves
- Intercostal Nerves
- Posterior & Lateral Cutaneous Nerves
- Superior Cluneal Nerves
- Superior Gluteal Nerve
- Inferior Gluteal Nerve
- Sciatic Nerve
- Posterior Femoral Cutaneous Nerve
- Gluteus Minimus
- Lateral Rotators

© Tracy Markley

# TIPPING TOWARD BALANCE

## CHAPTER THREE

# TRIPPING ON ROOTS AND FALLING

A 59-year-old male, approximately 50 pounds overweight, came to me because he needed to work on his balance. He explained to me that he was tripping and falling down often, especially while on his job, which required him to spend some of his work day walking on the hiking trails in the rainforest. Quite often he was going up and down hills but was unable to go very far due to foot pain, and he would often trip on the roots in the ground on the hiking trails. I agreed that he needed to train for better balance, as well as needing to regain the awareness of each foot's location in space.

Tripping on roots on a hiking trail is a great example of someone who is not connecting to the location of their feet in space. When he takes a step, his foot is not lifting high enough to step over the root, therefore he hits the root with his foot and trips. He does not have control of this, or awareness that he is doing it, it is just happening.

We met once a week to train, and a couple of days a week he would also do the exercises on his own. Within in a couple of weeks, he said he was not tripping anymore, nor had he fallen down.

He did the eight exercises listed in this book, plus he was able to add some battle ropes and other gentle exercises after a few months.

# TRIPPING ON ROOTS AND FALLING

# TIPPING TOWARD BALANCE

## CHAPTER FOUR

# BRUNS-GARLAND SYNDROME

A new 69-year-old male client came to me to build his upper body. He and I both laughed when he described that his wife jokingly told him that he was looking weak and unhealthy in the upper body and that he needed to get a personal trainer. He also told me that he was a diabetic. He had recently lost 60 pounds and had his diabetes under control. He also had peripheral neuropathy, tripping and falling often, especially when hiking on the forest trails. He then told me that he had Bruns-Garland Syndrome and that just months before, he had been in a wheelchair for several weeks, unable to walk.

I know most people reading this are probably asking, "What is that?" That was my question as well. He explained that it is a rare condition that mostly white males can develop with controlled diabetes. It affects the nerves in the low spine and paralyzes the legs. Some people don't recover from it and never walk again, but he did. However, it left him with a foot drop and atrophy in the leg on his left side.

> *Proximal neuropathy in diabetes mellitus (DM) is a condition in which patients develop severe aching or burning and lancinating pain in the hip and thigh. This is followed by weakness and wasting of the thigh muscles, which often occur asymmetrically. This disabling condition occurs in type 1 and type 2 DM. Bruns first described the disorder in patients with DM in 1890. [1] In 1955, Garland coined the term diabetic amyotrophy, although the*

*name Bruns-Garland syndrome is also used to describe the condition.*

(https://emedicine.medscape.com/article/1935459-overview)

He began training with me in one-hour sessions three days a week. We did free weights and specific exercises to strengthen the upper body, but we also added specific exercises to work on his core and balance. He needed to regain the awareness of the location of his feet in space.

Within just a couple months he was not falling down anymore when he hiked. His foot drop was less pronounced. He said that when his feet were in pain, they didn't hurt as badly as they did before the training began, and the pain did not last as long. He recently explained to me that he feels training with me helped cure the residual Bruns-Garland effects.

It is now over a year since we started training together. In the beginning, the leg that was affected by the Bruns-Garland Syndrome was atrophied and thinner than the other leg. Now his foot drop is 100% gone and both his legs are the same size.

**CHAPTER FIVE**

# FOOT PAIN AND FASCIAL ISSUES

This is a letter I received from a 47-year-old client with foot pain and joint pain throughout her body.

*Dear Tracy,*

*I've had pain in my feet off and on for thirty years (since I was about 18). Most recently the pain was so bad that it hurt to walk, especially in the morning. After working with you on the BOSU ball the pain has lessened significantly and most days I am completely pain free. It is hard to explain how much this has affected my life and how thankful I am. Then last week I was telling you about my hands and how stiff and painful my joints were in both hands. This has been happening off and on since I was a teenager. I have been tested for arthritis and have seen doctors for both my hands and feet. The medical community could never diagnose, so I had given up and would just wait for the flare ups (as I call them) to go away. The past several years the pain has been present more than it has been absent. You suggested we try a hand exercise on the BOSU ball. The results have been amazing. After the exercise the tips of my fingers tingled and after a few minutes I could feel tingling down my thumb joint and my first knuckle on my index finger. A day later I could bend my fingers! They had been so painful they were as stiff as pencils for weeks.*

## FOOT PAIN AND FASCIAL ISSUES

*Thank you for the work you do and the attention you give your clients and thank you to BOSU! What an amazing tool it is!*

*-Tammy*

When we began, she had balance issues because she was stiff in movement due to lack of activity and stress. She had been working 60 hours a week at a stressful job and was not exercising. She had quit that job and hired me as her trainer to help her get well.

Even though she was in her 40s, her body mimicked the limitations of clients I've trained who were over 70, with similar balance challenges. It appeared she had some fascial issues going on, along with tight muscles.

As she stood on the BOSU® Ball, her pain seemed to calm and the stiffness would begin to relax. I would have her stand on the BOSU® Ball with good posture, but not stiff posture. I would have her think calmness and relaxation and have her gently wiggle her fingers as she focused on NOT tightening the neck and shoulders.

She, like many, constantly kept her shoulders tight and lifted toward her ears. This keeps the neck and upper back muscles tense and tight as well as raising the shoulder joints out of proper alignment. Tight muscles and fascia in the neck and shoulder areas can lead to fascial issues throughout the body, including the feet.

As she focused on keeping her shoulders down and relaxed she was able to bring calmness to the pain throughout her body. She spent 5 to 10 minutes each session doing this as her warm up. Whenever she came in with joint pain in her hands and fingers, after this warm up the pain would fade away.

She would walk across the BOSU® Balls as in Exercise 6. Within a month of training with me she had no more foot pain.

## CHAPTER SIX

# Another Tripper

I began working with a wonderful 75-year-old female client. When we met, she told me that she was tripping and falling down more than she wished to. She also told me that her sister had dementia, and she was concerned about losing her memory. She also had hearing loss and wore hearing aids. She wanted to work on her balance. Like many others, she was not aware that strengthening the core and deep muscles in the spine would help with balance. Some people think that just practicing standing on one leg will train their body to balance. This is not true.

## TIPPING TOWARD BALANCE

She began training with me for 30-minute sessions, two days a week. After two months, she cut it down to one day a week. At that time, she began attending my special balance class which was held once a week for an hour. She bought a balance disc the first week we met and used it every day at home.

Within just a few weeks of working together, she stopped tripping and falling. She practiced daily and was soon able to add more exercises to her individual workouts. As of now she can stand on a BOSU® Ball and bounce a basketball, whereas in the beginning, she needed to hold onto a bar to stand on the BOSU® Ball. That is fantastic improvement at her age. Often, people think it is due to age that we become imbalanced, and it won't get better. That is not true.

CHAPTER SEVEN

# STROKE SURVIVORS

I have worked with dozens of stroke survivors, each one with their own level of challenges from their stroke. I am going to discuss two cases as examples of the way that the balance discs and BOSU® Balls play an essential role in recovery. The eight exercises included in this book greatly affect the neurological system, which is vital for recovery.

Stroke victims frequently experience spasticity. This condition causes a tight hand, and curled fingers, and often bent elbows. This stiffness makes it hard to use the hand for everyday movements, like picking up objects and grabbing a hold of something for safety.

## TIPPING TOWARD BALANCE

I was working with an 89-year-old male survivor with hand spasticity. He was two years post-stroke when I met him. He did not have very good balance, so we did much of his work sitting down, especially in the early training sessions.

I told him to concentrate on opening his hand with as much focus as he could give it. I even had him say the word "open" each time, as a verbal command, so that he was saying it, hearing it and physically trying to do it. It would open up about a quarter of an inch, then close right back up. I would have him open and close the other hand and look at it. I wanted him to feel and maintain a visual of what it is like for that hand to open up all the way with no challenges. I would have him do it with his eyes open, and with his eyes closed. I would then have him focus on the stroke-affected side again, and if he really focused, that hand would open up a little farther than that quarter of an inch.

Then one day I decided to have him try the exercise while standing on the balance disc. He had been using a balance disc and holding on for balance and brain stimulation exercises. I had him hold on with one hand and let the other hand hang by his side. I had him do the same exercise sequence he had been doing while seated. While standing on the disc he was able to open his stroke-affected hand almost two inches farther than when he was seated. When he stepped off the disc, the hand reverted back to its tighter curled up position. In the seventh training session, on the disc, his hand remained open when he stepped off the disc.

He only trained with me twice a week for 30-minute sessions. He did not practice at home. He had a hard time remembering to do things. I believe that if he had worked on this every day his results would have happened sooner, and he would have gained a much more advanced recovery in that hand.

Another client I trained was a 65-year-old male who had suffered a massive stroke, six months before we met. He was critical the first two weeks, and unable to move his body at all. The doctors were not sure if he was going to survive, but he beat the odds. I met him when he was six months post stroke, as he walked into the gym using a walker. He was the most fragile stroke survivor I have ever trained.

When he began he could not sit on the big exercise ball, but by the time he was two years post-stroke, he had achieved such great gains, we thought that this journey should be in a book. When he was about three years post-stroke, he was still achieving gains, and I had a hard time deciding where to end the book. He had just met and thanked the paramedics that saved his life on the day of his stroke, so we decided that would be a great way to end the book. Soon after we had made that decision, he was standing on the BOSU® Ball, and he said that the feeling had just completely come back into his leg. He is proof that there is no time frame for recovery.

He is an excellent example to stroke survivors that everyday physical activity, combined with specific exercises that stimulate the brain, help to rebuild those pathways. He did the eight exercises listed in this book almost daily. I could always find him in the gym balancing on the BOSU® Ball. He never gave up.

The book of his recovery was published in November 2017 and is called *The Stroke of An Artist: The Journey of a Fitness Trainer and a Stroke Survivor* by Tracy L. Markley.

## CHAPTER EIGHT

# Scoliosis

A 75-year-old female with scoliosis called me and said she had heard that I work with scoliosis. She told me her spine had developed scoliosis out of the blue about a year prior. She said that she never had it before, and that she had always moved easily with no problems.

She had tried everything possible to get her back straight again. She was able to ease some pain because someone had recommended a specific supplement product. She was grateful that it had helped her back pain to fade away.

## TIPPING TOWARD BALANCE

When we began working together she was anxious, and I could tell she was not feeling hopeful because, up until that moment, nothing had been working for her. We began standing on the BOSU® Ball to strengthen the postural muscles. If this worked, it could build the back muscles up to be more even, and therefore, help.

We did the exercises included in this book, and some others. Stretching was very important. Stretching the inner thighs, hips, quads, back, glutes, calves, and hamstrings all help to release the back.

She began coming to me two days a week for a couple of weeks, then she changed to one day a week. She was doing all the work we had done together on her own on the other days. I noticed that regardless of the stretches she did, her psoas muscle was not releasing. I told her that I thought she should see an acupuncturist in town who specialized in psoas releases. It appeared that this muscle was stopping the rest of the stretches from reaching their full potential. After the psoas release was done, she began to make better progress. The spine began to get straighter again.

# SCOLIOSIS

If a client needs to have a session with a massage therapist, acupuncturist or physical therapist, I will send them in that direction. I am so happy she went, otherwise she would have been limited with me. I could only have done so much because she could not have advanced to further exercises to strengthen the spine without this treatment.

I also have scoliosis. It runs in our family. When I was young and learning to walk the runway in modeling school, the teachers would tell me that something didn't look right, but they couldn't figure out what it was. When I discovered that I had scoliosis, I realized that it was making me look like I was not walking properly. Whenever I performed a squat in my twenties, I noticed that one of my hips would sway to one side. I thought at the time, that if I kept squatting like this I could end up wearing out that hip and end up with issues when I was older. I decided right then that I would do other exercises to work those muscles.

# TIPPING TOWARD BALANCE

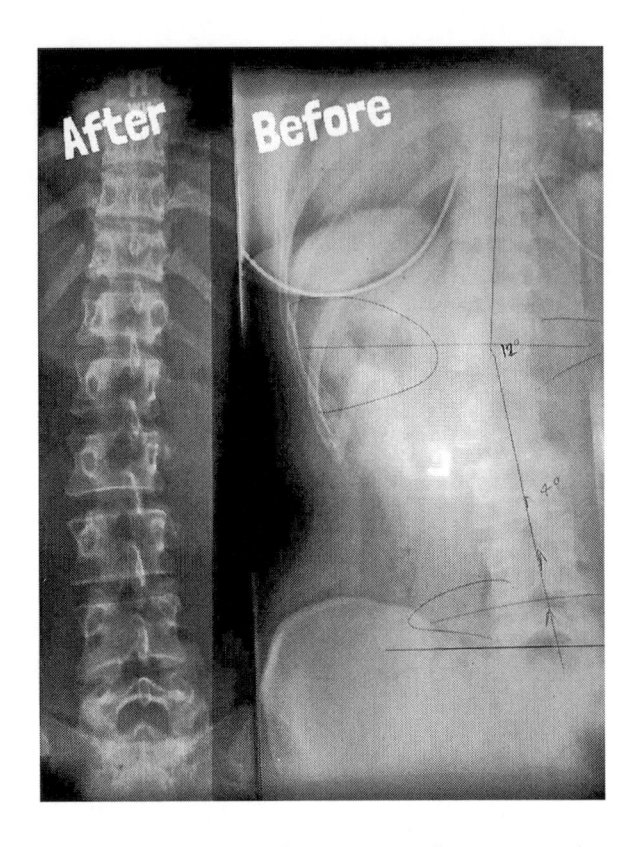

When I was in my late 20s, I began working on my core, and balancing, working with a disc, and the Swiss ball. I ended up decreasing the curve in my spine, but that was not my goal. I was not aware that this was happening until a year or so into doing the core exercises. I was actually feeling taller, so I went to the chiropractor/orthopedic office that was in the

# SCOLIOSIS

same building where my fitness studio was located. I told him what I felt, and I asked him if he would do another X-ray on me. He did, and we compared it to a previous one from five years earlier.

It's clear in the picture above that my spine had made a significant change. It had become straighter because of the core exercises I was doing.

Before my core muscles and deep spine muscles were strengthened, I could not walk farther than 5K, which is 3.1 miles. Each time I did events with a longer duration than that, one of my hips would be in pain the next day to the point where I could barely walk. I would have to go for a chiropractic adjustment, and spend a few weeks being extra careful.

Building a stronger spine and core, for me, has allowed me to be more active without pain. I am 52 years old now and I am pretty sure I would be on disability with chronic pain if I had let those muscles in the spine and core become weak and take control over me.

## TIPPING TOWARD BALANCE

Keep in mind, in my client's case, and indeed in my own case, we needed to do specific stretches that worked with our individual spine cases. Each person has specific stretches that may be better for them based on the individual curves in their spine.

The eight exercises in this book help greatly, but there are only some things you can do on your own. It is important, if possible, to find a qualified, knowledgeable professional to guide you through certain steps when needed. Always listen to your body.

**CHAPTER NINE**

# A LETTER FROM A 90-YEAR-OLD CLIENT

*I considered myself pretty healthy, for a 90-year-old. I played golf several times a week and was very active. Then I fell, twice.*

*I knew that falls can spell trouble for older adults. Although I'd taught skiing and been an avid skier earlier in my life, my balance had become iffy. I met Tracy when I took a yoga class from her. I thought I might be the only guy, but I was not. Some of the yoga positions were beyond me, but I thought Tracy was inspiring. After the second yoga class, Tracy suggested that I try her balance class. I was introduced to the BOSU ball, while holding onto a chair for stability. After several classes, I could step on and off the BOSU ball while maintaining my balance and felt pretty pleased with my progress. Tracy really worked with me on what she called my "spatial awareness" and bringing back my confidence in moving without falling. Tracy seemed genuinely interested in me and my progress; in addition to helping me with my balance, she took a broader interest in my health, such as encouraging me to drink more water.*

*She specializes in helping older adults who've had strokes, MS, Parkinson's, and other conditions that rob people of their balance and sense of security in their movement. Thank you for considering her for one of your fitness pros; I know others can benefit from her experience and wisdom.*

# A LETTER FROM A 90-YEAR-OLD CLIENT

This letter was written from my 90-year-old client who was nominating me for a personal trainer contest.

I noticed when he came to my yoga class that his balance was being challenged more than yoga could help. He attended my balance class one day a week for 10 weeks and did a few private personal training sessions with me. It's fascinating to see older clients gain back balancing skills. It makes me happy.

CHAPTER TEN

# 105 Years Old

When she was 104 1/4 years old, she joined the gym where I trained so that she could do private personal training sessions with me. She began coming in twice a week for 30 minutes. In one exercise, she would stand on a pink BOSU® ball and hold on to a bar in order to work on her balance and strengthening her postural muscles and core. When she got to the point where I thought it would be good for her to step up and down, forward and back, and side to side over the BOSU® Ball, I thought it would be a good idea for her to use a child-size BOSU® Ball. She began proudly walking through the parking lot

# TIPPING TOWARD BALANCE

and into the gym, caring her very own BOSU® ball on her walker. She even scanned her own key into the gym scanner each time she came in.

She learned to engage her core in order to help her stand up taller, and to help her balance both on the BOSU® Balls and as she walked. Within three months her posture underwent a big structural change. She focused on holding herself upright while she exercised

## 105 YEARS OLD

with me, and also on her own, when she was doing her everyday activities.

104 & 1/2 years young

104 & 2/3 years young

She did squats holding onto a bar while on the BOSU® ball, and even did pushups standing on the BOSU® Ball. A couple of times she let go with one hand on her own and whipped out a few one-arm pushups.

## TIPPING TOWARD BALANCE

She practiced walking backward and forward with her walker. She stayed aware of her body's location in space, and where she was placing her feet.

She was a wonderful example of being present and consistent when exercising, so that your body can make healthy changes at any age.

One day, when she had been training with me for about seven months, she needed to get an X-ray. Her daughter told me that when she was done, she sat up from the table without using her arms. The X-ray tech said excitedly, "She just sat up using her core!"

To read more of her story, see my blog at *http://tracys-healthy-365.blogspot.com.*

CHAPTER ELEVEN

# KIDS AND TEENS

These eight exercises are also great for kids and teens. They are a good base for sports training, and for those who feel shy or uncoordinated in sports and physical education classes. Feeling unbalanced or uncoordinated in physical activity can occur at any age.

I have trained with kids who are in the sport of ice skating and also kids in gymnastics, as well as kids who feel uncoordinated and dislike physical education classes. Women of all ages have told me they have been uncoordinated and clumsy their whole lives. They were those kids who used every excuse they could to get out of physical education classes because they felt they were unable to do what other kids in class could do.

On occasion in the last 20 years I have had mothers bring in their child to train with them to help them gain more confidence with their bodies and in physical activities. In some cases, this loss of confidence began from a negative comment that was said to them or from being teased.

A few years ago, I trained an 11-year-old girl who was a perfect example of a girl who hated physical education. She said she felt stupid and uncoordinated. We met two times a week for a few months. After the first month she told me that she participated in activities in her P.E. classes that she never would try before. She actually began to have fun in class, too.

The eight exercises in this book have helped people of all ages to gain better coordination from head to toe, leaving them feeling more confident to participate in physical education classes and sports. Kids and teens

# KIDS AND TEENS

also did more exercises than are mentioned in this book, because they could.

In the following pictures, a 5-year-old is having a fantastic time with all the colorful balls, balance discs and BOSU® balls, as he develops some great physical skills.

# TIPPING TOWARD BALANCE

**CHAPTER TWELVE**

# Hearing Loss Linked to Falls

Since this book is about preventing falls, I wanted to add that research has shown that hearing loss has also been linked to falls and dementia. Studies show that from the earliest months of life, hearing is intimately tied to the development of language, reading, learning, as well as cognitive and social skills. This is taken into adult life. When older adults lose their hearing, they can start losing their cognitive skills.

A study led by a Johns Hopkins researcher suggests that hearing loss is a risk factor for falls and every additional 10-decibels of hearing loss increased the chances of falling by 1.4 fold (https://www.healthyhearing.com/report/52548-New-research-links-hearing-loss-to-an-increased-risk-of-falls). The Hearing Health Foundation wrote that hearing loss is often linked with dementia, and research is being conducted to establish the exact link between the two. (https://www.hopkinsmedicine.org/news/media/releases/hearing_loss_linked_to_accelerated_brain_tissue_loss ). The research concluded that older adults with hearing loss tended to experience 30 to 40 percent accelerated cognitive dysfunction and were at a higher risk of developing dementia.

When someone first begins to wear hearing aids, the brain adjusts to them. This is normal. I know this very well because I wear hearing aids myself. If you need hearing aids and you only wear them occasionally, this can place you at a greater risk of falls.

I tell my older clients with hearing loss to get hearing aids if they need them, and if they have

## HEARING LOSS LINKED TO FALLS

hearing aids, to be sure to wear them consistently. It will help them greatly.

You can read more about hearing loss on my blog at *http://tracys-healthy-365.blogspot.com* and/or read about medical research linking hearing loss to falls.

CHAPTER THIRTEEN

# Balance Disc - BOSU® Ball - Swiss Ball

**Swiss Ball:**

The "Swiss Ball" was developed in 1963 by Aquilino Cosani, an Italian plastics manufacturer. A British physiotherapist used it in physical therapy in Switzerland. In the 1980's physical therapists brought the work to America, and soon it came into the fitness industry.

As years have passed the Swiss ball has been labeled as an exercise ball, a yoga ball, a therapy ball, and many other names. It is used for various exercises. I use it frequently in my workouts, and with clients. It is a ball that is big enough to sit on, as shown in the pictures.

Important points when using this ball:

- Have the ball at a height where your hips DO NOT drop below the knees.

- Be sure the ball is firm. You will not get proper spine support if the ball is squashy when you sit on it, or when you use it for exercises.

- Sit with your knees over the ankles (shins straight up and down). You don't want to sink into the knee joints as shown on pages 77 & 80.

- Always begin with caution. When first using the ball keep yourself near something to hold onto for safety.

## Balance Disc & BOSU® Ball:

I use the balance disc and BOSU® Ball with most clients. Balance discs are round, air-filled discs that

## BALANCE DISC - BOSU' BALL - SWISS BALL

are strong enough to sit, stand and exercise on. They are added to workouts to improve balance and increase core strength. The discs, and the BOSU® Ball, are considered unstable environments. They both challenge your balance and stimulate the central nervous system, which is the brain and spinal column. I use the 13-inch balance discs with my clients.

The balance disc is referred to as an unstable-stable environment, whereas the BOSU® Ball is referred to as a stable-unstable environment. It was scientifically invented to absorb the body's weight into its dome, allowing the bracing system in the body to relax. Therefore, the nerves are stimulated deeper into the nerve roots.

Both these tools are fantastic to use at any age for many great advantages. I feel they are essential to use with my clients in order to gain the best functioning body.

## Bender® Ball

This is a 9-inch inflatable plastic exercise ball. Other 9-inch balls are available and are often referred to as Pilates balls or small exercise balls. They usually all work. They come in a variety of rubber thicknesses. I have used the Bender® Ball for years, and I know exactly what I am getting when I place an order for myself or a client.

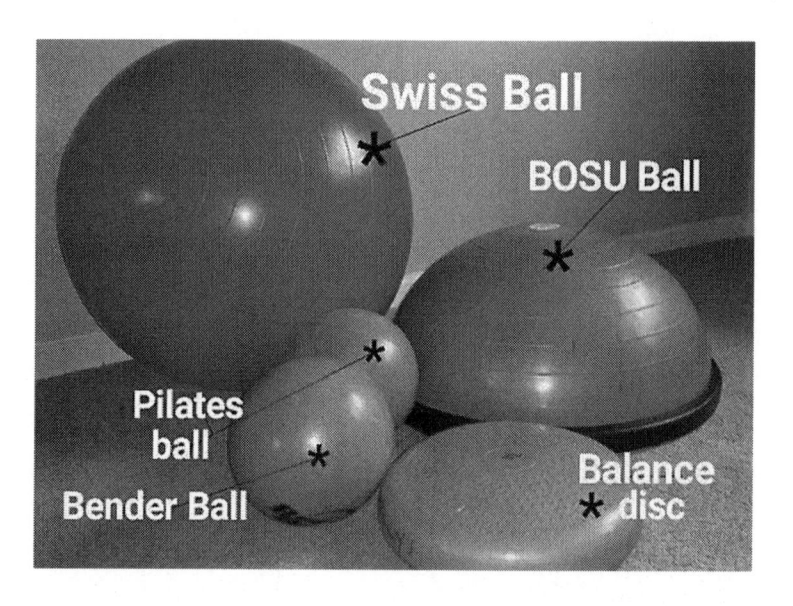

CHAPTER FOURTEEN

# EIGHT EXERCISES FOR BALANCE AND STABILITY IN MOVEMENT

Here are eight important exercises I have found essential to regaining balance, strength and stability for safe movement. Depending on the client, I may have him/her start by sitting on a Swiss ball, standing on the balance disc, or I may have the client start by standing on the BOSU® Ball. In all cases, especially in the beginning, I have the client hold on to a ballet barre or the squat rack bar even though I am in the fitness studio. If you are trying these at home, be sure to have a safe item to hold onto.

# TIPPING TOWARD BALANCE

In each standing exercise:

- Engage the core. Imagine you are zipping up a zipper to put on a snug girdle.

- Be aware of your body's location in space from head to toe.

- Be aware of foot placement. Feel them evenly anchored wherever you are standing. Try to keep feet evenly placed, don't let them roll out to the sides.

- Stand up tall, stack the shoulders over the hips, and imagine you are lengthening your spine to the sky.

- Imagine your body weight is lifting up, as the feet maintain the sense of being anchored in the ground.

- For safety, if needed, hold onto a bar or secure object, which allows you to maintain a good posture.

## FOR BALANCE AND STABILITY IN MOVEMENT

- Hold on enough to be safe, but don't become so stiff that you don't feel the balancing challenge of the disc or BOSU® Ball.

- If you are sitting on the stability (Swiss) ball, anchored as described above, keep the knees over the ankles, and sit up tall with your shoulders over your hips.

- Follow the instructions and tips listed with each of the following exercises.

---

*The information in this book is not intended to replace the advice of your physician. It's best to consult your physician before starting any exercise program. You should consult your doctor regarding any medical condition which concerns you. The material in this book is intended to inform and educate the reader. Neither the author nor the publisher assumes any responsibility or liability for the judgments or decisions any reader might make as a result of reading this publication.*

## Exercise 1

## *Sitting on a Stability (Swiss) Ball*

- Be sure the ball is firm

- Be sure the ball is the right height for you. (Your hips should be level with your knees. Do not sit on a squashy ball, or on a ball where your hips are below your knees.)

- Sit on the ball so that your legs are as close to the ball as they can be without touching the ball.

- Keep your knees directly over your ankles. This means your shin bone will be in a straight line, from the ankle to the knee. Think of table legs coming directly out of the table joint, which allows the table leg to be positioned straight up and down.

- Don't let your knees fall in or fall out, and don't squeeze your legs together.

## FOR BALANCE AND STABILITY IN MOVEMENT

- Anchor your feet into the floor.

- Engage your pelvic floor (if possible), without engaging the glutes (squeezing your butt muscles).

- Engage your core like you are putting on a snug girdle.

- Stack your shoulders over the hips.

In the beginning, you may feel that there are too many things to remember. That is okay, it is normal. Keep focusing from head to toe. This will help the body and brain regain better communication consciously, which will help rebuild the communication subconsciously, as you strengthen the muscles in your spine and core.

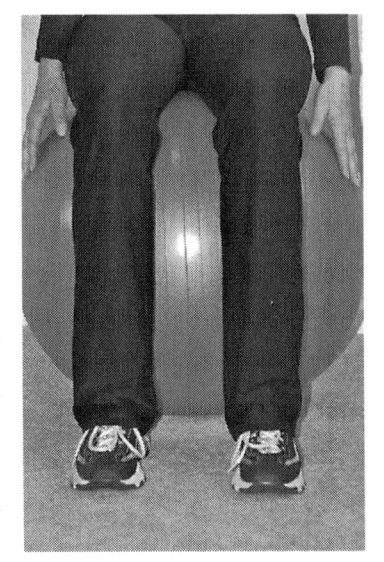

## Exercise 2

## *Sitting on a Stability (Swiss) Ball - Adductor/Abductor Exercise*

Use a Bender® Ball or a small soft Pilates ball, and gently squeeze between the knees/inner thighs. This can be done with your feet flat on the floor and on tip toes.

- Set up your position on the ball (as in Exercise 1).

- Place the ball between your knees or inner thighs, wherever it feels comfortable for you.

- Check your position and posture again and envision yourself putting on that girdle (as in Exercise 1).

- Gently but firmly squeeze the ball between your knees (inner thighs), with control, then release, with control. Repeat this movement for 10 to 20 reps. Be sure to use the same speed

## FOR BALANCE AND STABILITY IN MOVEMENT

throughout the exercise. (Try NOT to squeeze the ball, and then quickly snap the release.) Work yourself up to three sets of 20 reps. This number changes and varies per person. When I am working with a client, we communicate and determine the number that works for them based on the strength and ability of the client.

- Do NOT engage the glutes (squeeze the buttocks) while performing this exercise. For most people, this takes the focus.

- As with any exercises, if your back, hip or knee joints hurt while doing this exercise, first recheck your form and if that does not fix it, STOP the exercise!

- It is never a good idea to hurt one area of the body in order to strengthen another. Proper exercise that works the whole body while avoiding injuries is essential.

TIPPING TOWARD BALANCE

80

## Exercise 3

# *Standing on the Balance Disc*

It is important to have a balance disc that is not too flimsy. I have found that the CanDo® brand 35cm/13 inch is a good one to use.

- Engage the core. Imagine you are zipping up a zipper to put on a snug girdle before even stepping onto the balance disc. Re-engage once you are standing on the balance disc.

- Be aware of the body's location in space from head to toe.

- Be aware of the placement of your feet. Feel them evenly anchored where you are standing. Try to keep your feet evenly placed and don't let them roll out to the sides.

- Wear shoes or be barefoot. I suggest shoes in the beginning, they add more support. Don't wear just socks - that can risk slipping.

# TIPPING TOWARD BALANCE

- Stand up tall, stack your shoulders up over your hips and imagine you are reaching the top of your head to the sky.

- Imagine your body weight is lifting up as your feet maintain the sense of being anchored to the ground.

- Hold onto a bar or secure object so you can maintain a good posture, but don't hold the body so stiff that you don't feel the balancing challenge of the disc.

- Practice 3-5 minutes of balancing, one to five times a day.

- Depending on your individual balance strength or challenges, you have to begin at your own level.

FOR BALANCE AND STABILITY IN MOVEMENT

Engage Abs like you're putting on a girdle.

Keep feet horizontal. Don't let heels or toes touch the ground.

Face and hold onto a bar if needed.

# TIPPING TOWARD BALANCE

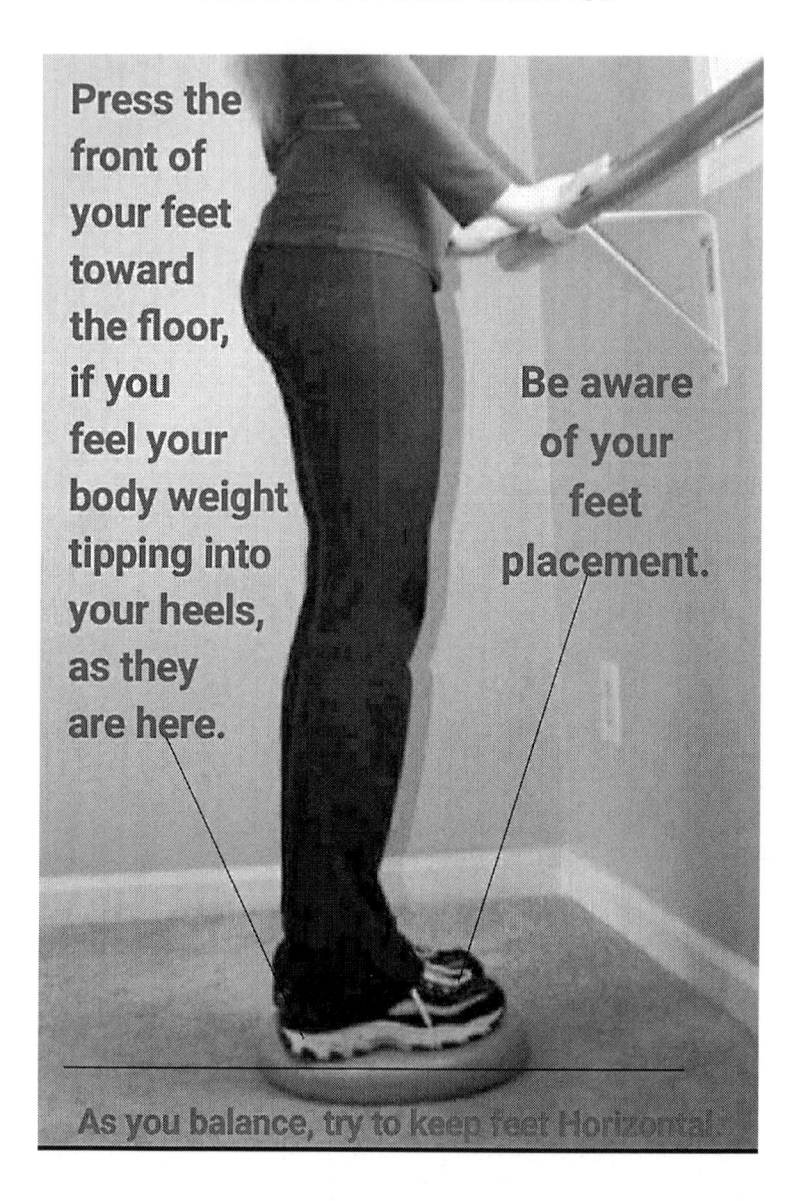

Press the front of your feet toward the floor, if you feel your body weight tipping into your heels, as they are here.

Be aware of your feet placement.

As you balance, try to keep feet Horizontal.

## Exercise 4

## *Standing on the BOSU® Ball*

It is important that you have the BOSU® Ball, inflated to its proper firmness. Usually, if you turn the BOSU® Ball over so that the platform is facing up and measure the distance from the floor to the top of the platform, it should be about 9 to 10 inches off the ground. I have noticed that BOSU® Balls can vary a bit in size. A flatter ball DOES NOT MEAN IT'S A BETTER CHALLENGE. That is not how it works. It is not the science behind this piece of equipment.

- Engage the core. Imagine you are zipping up a zipper to put on a snug girdle before even stepping up from the floor. Re-engage once, standing on the BOSU® Ball.

- Be aware of your body's location in space from head to toe.

- Be aware of foot placement. Feel them evenly anchored to where you are standing. Try to keep your feet evenly placed, and don't let them roll out to the sides.

- Stand up tall, stack your shoulders up over your hips and imagine you are reaching the top of your head to the sky.

- Imagine that your body weight is lifting up as your feet maintain the sense of being anchored.

- Hold onto a bar or secure object so that you can maintain good posture, but don't hold the body so stiff that you don't feel the balancing challenge of the BOSU® Ball.

- Practice 3-5 minutes of balancing, one to five times a day.

- Depending on your individual balance strength or challenges, you have to begin at your own level.

## FOR BALANCE AND STABILITY IN MOVEMENT

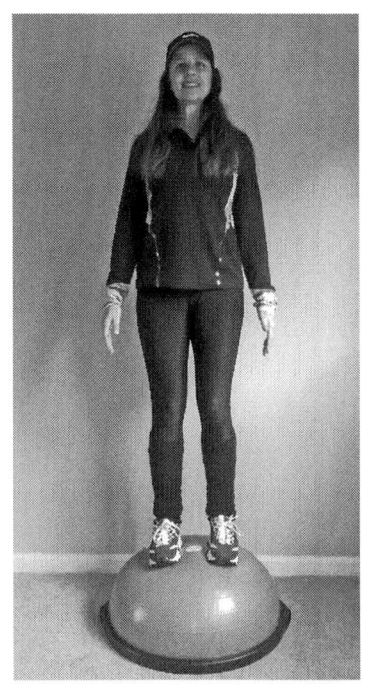

**Be aware of feet placement.**

## Exercise 5

## *Stepping on and off the BOSU® Ball*

- Engage as explained in Exercise 1 or for the balance disc before even stepping on to the dome of the BOSU® Ball.
- Spend a few minutes standing and balancing.
- When you are ready to step up and down, remind yourself to stay focused, and mindful of each individual foot's placement as you step up and step down.
- Come to a complete balance once both feet are on the dome. Stand up tall, stacking your shoulders over your hips.
- When you feel balanced, stay focused and then step back to the floor.
- Once you come to a complete balance on the floor, stand up tall, stacking your shoulders over your hips, then step back onto the dome.

## FOR BALANCE AND STABILITY IN MOVEMENT

- If possible, begin by stepping up with the right foot and stepping down with the right foot. Do this five times; then switch to stepping up with the left foot and stepping down with the left foot.

- Work yourself up to 10 on each side.

- If you personally have a foot drag, a drop challenge, or another physical challenge or weakness making this difficult to do, *KEEP PRACTICING. I*t will get easier with time. *The more you are receptive to a movement, the better chance the brain has of making the new pathway needed for such a movement.*

- When stepping off to the floor, focus on clearing the dome. Don't let your foot drag down the dome or hit the plastic platform. If you have extra physical challenges, this movement will come with time. *KEEP PRACTICING.*

- When finished with stepping up and down, go back to just standing and balancing. You will find you can balance better now. If the first few times you don't experience this, it will come with time. *KEEP PRACTICING.*

This is a very important exercise to help you regain balance and rebuild a safe and strong walking gait. It helps to rebuild an awareness of the location of your feet in space during your movement.

We take small steps stepping backwards many times each day:

- When we open a door towards us,
- When we approach a chair to sit down,
- Doing laundry,
- Stepping down a ladder or step,
- Backing away from the bathroom or kitchen sink,
- Using your feet to push yourself in a chair away from a table before you stand, and more.

## FOR BALANCE AND STABILITY IN MOVEMENT

*If you are having a hard time with the exercise of walking backwards, begin with Exercise 5 first, and/or include it in your workout program before you work on walking backwards.*

***Remember, the brain sends a message to the deep core muscles to stabilize the body before movement; Exercise 5 will help rebuild the body's natural system of flow for stepping and walking backward.***

# TIPPING TOWARD BALANCE

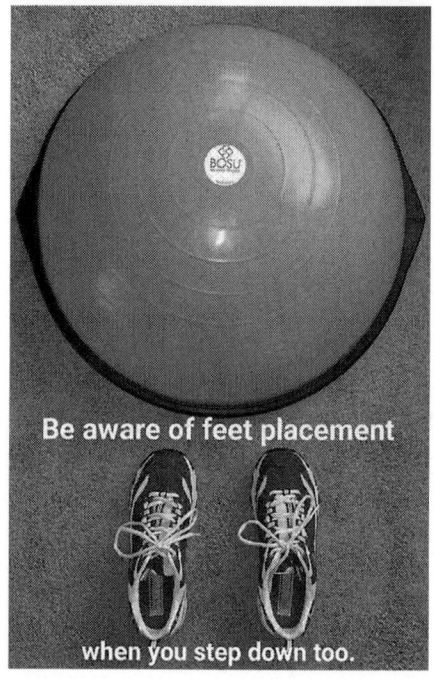

Be aware of feet placement.

Be aware of feet placement when you step down too.

FOR BALANCE AND STABILITY IN MOVEMENT

## Exercise 6

## *Walking Across 3 or more BOSU® Balls*

**This is more advanced. Only do this exercise when you are stable enough to do it!**

- Begin with placing the BOSU® Balls in a straight line next to a barre. Use a ballet barre or a squat rack bar at the gym that holds the rack securely in place or use something secure.

- Hold on safely with one hand, facing the end of the row of domes.

- Engage your core, and be aware of your body from head to toe as explained in previous exercises.

- When you are ready, step up on the first dome.

- Find your balance and stand up tall, staying engaged.

## TIPPING TOWARD BALANCE

- When ready, safely step from the first dome onto the second dome.

- When you are balanced and feel in control, safely step onto the third dome.

- Find your balance again, and when feeling safe and in control, step off the dome onto the floor.

- Turn around and repeat, going in the other direction. (You are now holding on with the other hand.)

- Depending on each individual, if you are more challenged on one side and are having a hard time holding on with a particular hand, do not walk on domes in that direction until you feel safe, and/or have a therapist or qualified professional with you.

- Try stepping from one dome to the next, leading with the right foot for some steps. Then do the same, leading with the left foot.

## FOR BALANCE AND STABILITY IN MOVEMENT

- Start focused, try to control the step of each foot and place it exactly where you want it to be.

- Do not randomly land your foot anywhere. Work on controlling your step.

- *Advanced.* **If** and **only when** you are ready, instead of stepping on to the floor to turn around, turn around on the last dome very slowly, with very small steps and with control.

- *Advanced.* **If** and **only when** you are ready, walk across the domes without holding onto a barre/bar. Remember, it is not necessary to do this without holding onto something in order to achieve results.

# TIPPING TOWARD BALANCE

Holding onto bar.

## FOR BALANCE AND STABILITY IN MOVEMENT

## Exercise 7

# *Walking Backward*

<u>Only practice walking backward if you can safely to do so</u>.

You can walk alongside a bar, or something to hold onto if needed.

If you do not have control of placing each foot exactly where you want it when you step, <u>walking backwards will not be safe for you. Safety first.</u>

After doing the previous exercises for some time, the ability to walk backward will feel safe again.

Once you are ready to walk backward, find a safe area. I find it is best to have a mirror in front of you to watch yourself, but this is not always an available option.

If you are having a hard time with the exercise of walking backwards, begin with Exercise 5 first, and/or

## FOR BALANCE AND STABILITY IN MOVEMENT

include it in your workout program before you work on walking backwards.

<u>If you are using a walker, DO THIS ONLY in a safe space with someone guiding you</u>.

## Exercise 8

## *Squats Holding on to a Bar*

This exercise can be done standing on the floor or standing on the BOSU® Ball.

- Begin by doing this exercise with your feet on the floor first, to be sure you can hold the proper alignment safely before you begin performing this on the dome of the BOSU® Ball.

- While facing the bar, evenly hold onto the bar with your hands so that your body is centered between your hands.

- Engage your core and focus. Hold the body in good form from head to toe, including the shoulders.

- Sit back as if you are going to sit in a chair, then raise yourself back up.

- Try to use your legs and glutes to do the movement. Don't allow the arms to do all the

## FOR BALANCE AND STABILITY IN MOVEMENT

work. Press your feet into the floor or dome as you come up.

- Do not drop the hips below the knees.

- If this bothers your knees, check your form. If it still bothers your knees do not do the exercise.

- If you are doing this standing on the floor, pull yourself up to a good posture between each squat.

- If you are doing this on the dome, pull yourself up to good posture, and balance yourself straight up and down in good form between each squat.

- Maintain control and focus throughout each movement.

- In each squat, make sure both feet are parallel, so that your hips and pelvis are moving evenly through both sides throughout each rep.

- If you are using the BOSU® Ball, do about 8-10 squats, then spend a couple of minutes

## TIPPING TOWARD BALANCE

balancing on the dome. When you are stronger, work up to three sets of 10 squats, balancing in between.

- Work your way up to the squatting. Depending on each individual, you may not feel safe to do the squats in the first few weeks.

# FOR BALANCE AND STABILITY IN MOVEMENT

Practice walking forward every day. Practice all of these exercises daily if you can. Listen to your body, and its guidance.

These are the basic exercises used with all the clients whose stories I've shared throughout this book. If you jumped straight to the exercise chapter of this book and skipped the stories of the client's journeys, I encourage you strongly to go back and read each story.

## TIPPING TOWARD BALANCE

The body needs to heal. Each person's body heals at its own pace. Try to be patient and respect your own body. Be kind to yourself.

When you feel ready to add some free weights, you can sit on the Swiss Ball, stand on the disc, stand on the BOSU® Ball or even kneel on the BOSU® Ball and do bicep curls, shoulder raises or other upper body exercises in proper form. I don't suggest doing overhead exercises when you are using these unstable surfaces. It can put pressure on your spine.

Stay safe.

# ACKNOWLEDGEMENTS

I would like to express my gratitude to supportive friends and parents who have been by my side through my personal training journey. Thank you to Greg Justice and Kelli O'Brien Watson for teaching me about book publishing and teaming up with me in creating the book design.

A big thank you to all my clients who trust and believe in my work. Thank you for being committed to your workouts with consistency and dedication, to achieve strong results.

*Tracy is available for speaking events, workshops, private and group training, in person or via internet.*

*Contact Tracy through the "Contact Tracy" page at her website.*
**www.tracyspersonaltraining.com**

# The Body Was Made to Move!

# Keep Moving!

# Don't Quit!

# Don't Give Up!

# ALSO FROM AMAZON BESTSELLING AUTHOR, TRACY L. MARKLEY

*"Read this book! It will encourage you to overcome any obstacle you may face and help you to help others to keep on keeping on!"*
-Diana M. De Paul

*Available on Kindle and in paperback at [www.tracyspersonaltraining.com](www.tracyspersonaltraining.com) and on Amazon.*

*Also available in audio at [Audible.com](Audible.com) and in iTunes*

Printed in Great Britain
by Amazon